THE ULTIMATE DVD
READ AND SHARE
Bible
VOLUME ONE

For:
DAVID BROOKS STELK

From:
MOMMY

Date:
AUGUST 13, 2011

Give thanks to the Lord and pray to him.
Tell the nations what he has done.
Sing to him. Sing praises to him.
Tell all the wonderful things he has done.
Be glad that you are his.
Let those who ask the Lord for help be happy.
Depend on the Lord and his strength.
Always go to him for help.
Remember the wonderful things he has done.
Remember his miracles and his decisions. . . .
He will keep his promises always.

PSALM 105:1–5, 8

THE ULTIMATE DVD READ AND SHARE® Bible

VOLUME ONE

More Than 100 Best-Loved
Bible Stories

Stories Retold by
Gwen Ellis

Illustrated by Steve Smallman

Tommy NELSON®

A Division of Thomas Nelson Publishers

NASHVILLE   DALLAS   MEXICO CITY   RIO DE JANEIRO

The Ultimate DVD Read and Share® Bible
© 2007, 2010 by Tommy Nelson, a Division of Thomas Nelson, Inc.

Published in Nashville, Tennessee, by Tommy Nelson.
Tommy Nelson is a registered trademark of Thomas Nelson, Inc.

Stories based on *The Holy Bible, International Children's Bible*®, copyright © 1986, 1988, 1999, 2005 by Thomas Nelson, Inc.

Stories retold by Gwen Ellis
Illustrated by Steve Smallman

Thomas Nelson titles may be purchased in bulk for educational, business, fund-raising, or sales promotional use. For information, please e-mail SpecialMarkets@ThomasNelson.com.

ISBN 978-1-4003-1613-7 (Volume One)

Library of Congress Cataloging-in-Publication Data
Ellis, Gwen.
    The ultimate DVD read and share Bible : more than 100 best-loved Bible stories /
  stories retold by Gwen Ellis ; illustrated by Steve Smallman.
       p. cm.
    "Stories based on the Holy Bible, International Children's Bible"—T.p. verso.
    ISBN 978-1-4003-1613-7 (v.1 : hardback) 1. Bible stories, English. I. Smallman, Steve.
  II. Title.
  BS551.3.E56 2010
  220.9'505—dc22   2010018908

Mfr.: RR Donnelley / Shenzhen, China / July 2010 / PPO # 109127

Stories on DVD 1

The Beginning—*Six Days of Creation*
Adam and Eve—*Sneaky Snake; Out of the Garden*
The Flood—*Noah's Big Boat; Animals Inside; The Dove; The Rainbow*
Abram—*Promised Land; Abraham's Visitors; Sarah Laughs; Baby Isaac*
Isaac and Rebekah—*A Wife for Isaac; Water for the Camels; Rebekah*
Jacob and Esau—*The Twins; Sneaky Jacob; Foolish Esau*
Rachel—*A Ladder to Heaven; Rachel; Tricked by Laban*
Home Again—*Jacob Wrestles with God; Jacob and Esau Meet*
John the Baptist—*Angel's Message; A Baby Named John;*
    John Baptizes Jesus
Jesus Is Born—*Mary's Big Surprise; Joseph Marries Mary;*
    Sleepy Shepherds; Gifts for Baby Jesus
Jesus Tempted by Satan—*Stones to Bread; Top of the Temple;*
    Kingdoms of the World
Jesus Loves Children—*Healing a Sick Boy; Bringing a Girl Back to Life;*
    Loaves & Fishes
One Lost Sheep—*A Son Spends His Money; Eating Pig's Food;*
    Home to Father

Stories on DVD 2

Gideon—*Gideon; Too Many Soldiers; Trumpets & Pots*
Samson—*Delilah; Samson's Haircut; Pushing the Pillars*
Ruth & Naomi—*Ruth Gathers Grain; Ruth and Boaz*
Hannah—*Hannah's Prayer; Hannah's Boy*
Samuel—*Samuel Listens; The Holy Box; Coming Home; Thunderclap*
David & the Giant—*Youngest Son; The Shepherd; Down Goes the Giant*
David Is Chased—*King Saul Chases David; Jonathan; Jonathan's Son*
Elijah—*2 Kingdoms; King Ahab; Whose God Is Real?; Fire From Heaven*
Esther—*A Beautiful Queen; Angry Haman; Esther Saves Her People*
Shadrach, Meshach, Abednego—*3 Brave Men; The Extra Man*
Saul Becomes Paul—*A Mean Man; Saul Is Blinded; Ananias Helps Saul*
Paul's Travels—*A Woman Who Sold Purple Cloth; Earthquake!*
Paul's Shipwreck—*People Laugh at Paul; Shipwrecked!;*
    A Poisonous Snake

Contents

New Testament Stories   149

The First Day

Genesis 1:1–5

In the beginning God made heaven and
earth. At first it was empty and dark.
But God gathered up the light and called
it *day*.

Then He gathered up the darkness and called it *night*. God was watching over everything.

What do you think God did next?

The Second Day

Genesis 1:6–8

On day two God divided the air from the water. He put some water above the air and some below it. He named the air *sky*.

The next day God made something many children like, especially in the summer. Can you guess what it is?

5

The Third Day

Genesis 1:9–13

On day three God was busy. He made puddles and oceans and lakes and waterfalls and rivers. He made the dry ground too.

Next He made plants. He made so many different kinds of trees, flowers, and bushes, that no one could count them all. God said His work was good.

Wow! God made so much on that day.
But can you guess what was missing?

The Fourth Day

Genesis 1:14–19

On day four God put the sun in the sky to
warm the earth. He saw that the night
was very dark, so God put the moon and
the stars in the sky.

8

Then God made spring, summer, fall, and winter. All that He made was good.

Next God made flippy, flappy fun things.
Let's see what they were.

The Fifth Day

Genesis 1:20–23

On day five God made starfishes, octopuses, whales, and turtles. He made fast little fish for rivers and slippery big fish for the ocean.

10

He made big birds like eagles to soar in the sky and zippy little birds like hummingbirds. He made birds in all shapes, sizes, and colors.

Which bird do you think is the prettiest?
Which is the strongest?

The Sixth Day

Genesis 1:24–31

On day six God made the animals—
puppies, cows, horses, kitties, bears,
lizards, mice, worms, and lots more.
Everything was good.

But something was still missing. There were no people. So God made some. And when He made them, He made them like Himself. He made them so they could be friends with Him.

Where do you think the first people lived?

Adam and Eve

Genesis 2:1–5, 15–22; 3:20

God named the first man Adam. God put Adam in a beautiful garden. He gave him all the animals. He gave him all the fish and the birds too.

Then God gave Adam one more thing.
God made a woman to be Adam's wife.
Adam named his wife Eve. On day seven
God rested from all His work.

**Uh-oh. Something bad was about
to happen on the earth.**

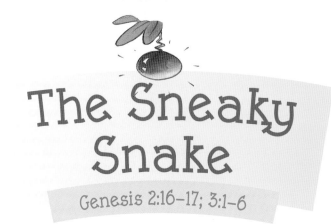

The Sneaky Snake

Genesis 2:16–17; 3:1–6

God gave Adam and Eve one rule. "Eat anything you like except the fruit from the tree in the middle of the garden."

A sneaky old snake came to Eve. "Eat it, then you'll know everything, just like God." So Eve ate the fruit and gave some to Adam. And he ate it too.

When we disobey God, it's called *sin*. There are always consequences when we disobey.

Out of the Garden

Genesis 3:8–24

One evening God came to visit Adam and Eve. But they were hiding. When God found them, He asked, "What have you done?" Adam told God everything. God was sad.

Because they had disobeyed God, Adam and Eve had to leave the beautiful garden. When they were outside of the garden, Adam and Eve had to work very hard to grow food.

It makes God very sad when we disobey.
It makes our parents sad too.

Noah

Many years later there were lots of people on the earth, but most of them were bad. One man—Noah—was good. He obeyed God. "I want you to build a boat," God told Noah.

Noah started right away. People laughed at Noah because they lived in a desert and there was no water for his boat. Noah just went on building the boat.

21

Do you think it is easy to obey when everyone is laughing at you?

The Big Boat

Genesis 7:1–15

When the boat was finished, God told Noah and his family to go into the boat. In went his sons Shem, Ham, and Japheth. In went their wives and Mrs. Noah.

"Now bring two of every animal," God told Noah. Noah did exactly what God told him to do. And God watched over him.

Something very wet was about to happen outside.

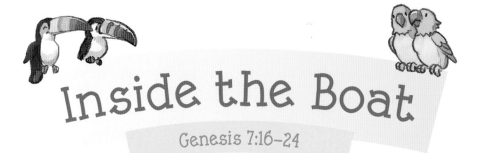

Inside the Boat

Genesis 7:16–24

When the last animal climbed into the boat, God shut the door. *Plip! Plop! Plip!* It began to rain. It rained so much, the water was over the meadows. It rained so much, it covered the towns. It rained so much, it even covered the mountains.

But inside the boat, everyone was safe.

How many days do you think it rained?

The Dove

Genesis 7:12; 8:1–19

After 40 days and 40 nights, the rain stopped, but it still wasn't time to get off the boat. Water was everywhere. One day Noah let a little dove fly out to see what was happening on the earth.

It brought a green leaf back. Hooray!
The plants were growing again! It was
almost time to come out!

**What do you think everyone did when Noah
opened the door of the boat?**

The Rainbow

Genesis 8:18–22; 9:1–17

When everyone was out of the boat, Noah built an altar. He thanked God for keeping them safe. Then something wonderful happened!

28

God put a beautiful rainbow in the sky and made Noah a promise. "It will never flood over the whole earth like that again," God said. When God makes a promise, He keeps it.

All God's promises are in the Bible. Isn't it wonderful to think of all He has promised us?

Babel

Genesis 11:1–9

Many years later there were lots of
people on the earth. They all spoke the
same language. Some people who lived in
the city of Babel became too proud. "Let's
build a tower that reaches to the sky.
We'll be famous."

God caused them to speak different languages so they couldn't talk to one another. Because they couldn't understand one another, they stopped building the tower.

31

Do you have any friends who speak a foreign language? Are you patient with them?

Abram

Genesis 12:1–3; 15:5; 22:17

God picked Abram to be the father of
a very important family. One day in
the future, Jesus would come from this
family.

God told Abram, "I will make you famous. Your children and grandchildren will be as many as the stars. They will be as many as the grains of sand on the beach. You won't be able to count them."

Wow! That's a wonderful promise. How do you think Abram felt?

Promised Land

Genesis 12:1–9

God told Abram to move to a new place. Abram had no map. God said, "I will show you where to go." Abram started out walking. He took his wife, nephew, and servants with him.

When Abram and his family got to a land called Canaan, God said, "This is your new home. I am giving it to you and to everyone who will ever be in your family."

If your parents said, "We're going on a trip, but we can't tell you where," would you trust them to take you to a good place?

Abraham's Visitors

Genesis 17:1–8; 18:1–8

When Abram was 99 years old, God changed his name to Abraham. His new name showed that he belonged to God. Not long after that, three men came by Abraham's tent, and he invited them to lunch.

"Quick! Bake some bread," Abraham told his wife. Then Abraham hurried to get some meat cooked. When the food was ready, Abraham brought it to his visitors. The men sat down to eat.

Abraham didn't know it,
but his visitors were from heaven.

Sarah Laughs

Genesis 18:9–16

When one of the visitors finished
eating, he said, "Where is your wife,
Sarah?" "She's over there in the tent,"
Abraham said. "Next year Sarah will
have a baby," the visitor said.

Sarah heard and laughed. She couldn't believe it. *I'm too old to have a baby, she* thought. *Abraham is too old too.*

What if your great-grandmother had a baby? Sarah was that old. Let's see how God keeps His promises.

Baby Isaac

Genesis 21:1–7

In about a year Sarah had a baby boy, just like God had promised. Abraham named the baby Isaac. Isaac means "laughter."

Sarah was so happy with her baby boy.
She said, "God has made me laugh.
Everyone who hears about this will
laugh with me."

**God can do anything, but sometimes it takes
a while to see the answer. What would you like
to ask Him to do for you?**

A Wife for Isaac

Genesis 24:1–14

Many years later, Isaac was all grown up. "Go back to the land I came from and find a wife for my son," Abraham said to his servant.

The servant loaded up camels with all kinds of wonderful presents. After he got to the land far away, he wasn't sure how to find a wife for Isaac. At a place where girls came to get water, he prayed, "Let the right girl give me water."

How many jugs of water do you think those camels could drink?

Water for the Camels

Genesis 24:15–20

Before the servant had finished praying, a beautiful young woman came to get water. The servant asked her, "Will you give me some water, please?"

44

"Yes," she said. "I'll get water for your camels too." It was a big job. Thirsty camels can drink a lot of water. Back and forth she went, pouring water for them all.

45

Do you think the man noticed how kind the woman was?

Rebekah

Genesis 24:21–61

The servant knew this woman was the one to be Isaac's wife. Her name was Rebekah. The servant took gifts to her family and asked if Rebekah could marry Isaac.

Her father said she could, and Rebekah wanted to get married too. So she went home with the servant to meet Isaac.

The servant needed God to help him find the right girl. What do you do when you need God's help?

Isaac and Rebekah

Genesis 24:62–67

The camels swayed and bumped along the road all the way to Canaan where Isaac lived. One evening just before the sun went down, the camels stopped.

A young man was walking in the field. He looked up and saw the camels. His bride had come. Isaac loved Rebekah. He married her.

Do you think Rebekah was excited about being chosen to be Isaac's wife? How do you think she felt about going so far away?

The Twins

Genesis 25:21-26

For many years Rebekah couldn't have babies. So Isaac prayed to God about the problem. God heard Isaac, and He sent *two* babies—twins. When the twins were born, one was all red and fuzzy. Isaac and Rebekah named him Esau.

The other twin had smooth skin. They named him Jacob. Someday, when they were grown up, these boys would be the leaders of two great families.

God has the answers to all our prayers.
What would you like to pray about?

Sneaky Jacob

Genesis 25:27-34

The boys grew up, and one day Esau came in from hunting. Jacob was cooking. "I'm hungry. Give me some of that soup!" said Esau.

Jacob was a sneaky guy. He said, "Give me your rights as the firstborn son, and I will." Esau agreed, "Okay. If I starve, my rights won't help me."

Esau made a bad decision. Pray and ask God to help you make good decisions.

Foolish Esau

Genesis 25:34; 27:1-37

Jacob gave Esau a big bowl of soup, and he ate it. Esau didn't even know he had been tricked.

Later on Esau found out what that bowl of soup cost him. Isaac, their father, gave everything he had to Jacob when it should have been Esau's. Esau had been foolish.

Esau thought he had to have something right now. Why is it foolish *not* to think about consequences?

A Ladder to Heaven

Genesis 27:41–46; 28:10–18

When Esau found out how Jacob had tricked him, he was mad. Jacob was afraid and ran away from him. That night in the desert, Jacob had to sleep outside with a rock under his head for a pillow.

56

He dreamed about a ladder to heaven filled with angels. God spoke to Jacob in the dream and promised to bless him.

What do you think it would be like to have a rock for a pillow?

Rachel

Genesis 29:1–20

Jacob continued his journey, traveling
a long way to his uncle Laban's house.
There he met Laban's beautiful daughter
Rachel. Jacob fell in love with her.

He told Laban, "I'll stay here and work for you if you'll let me marry Rachel." So Jacob stayed and worked seven years for the woman he loved.

Is there anything you'd be willing to wait seven years for?

Tricked!

Genesis 29:21-24

After seven years of hard work, it was finally time for Jacob's wedding. Everyone got dressed. The bride wore a heavy veil over her face. It was so heavy that Jacob couldn't see through it.

Guess what? Laban tricked Jacob. Rachel was not under the veil. It was her sister, Leah, instead.

How do you think Jacob felt when he found out he had been tricked?

Home Again

Genesis 29:25–30; 31:1–55

Jacob was mad at Laban. "What have you done?" Jacob asked. Laban said, "Work some more, and I'll give you Rachel too." Jacob married Rachel and worked seven more years.

Then Jacob decided to leave Rachel's sneaky father. He took his family and everything he had and started back home.

Jacob was going home, but that's where his angry brother, Esau, lived. What do you think happened when they met?

Jacob Wrestles with God

Genesis 32:26–28

When Jacob was almost home, a servant said, "Your brother, Esau, is coming." Jacob thought Esau was coming to hurt him. Jacob was afraid and prayed, "God, save me from my brother!"

That night a man, who was really God, appeared. Jacob wrestled with the man. "Bless me," Jacob said. God blessed Jacob and changed his name to Israel.

Jacob means "sneaky." *Israel* means "one who wrestles with God." Which kind of person would you rather be?

Jacob and Esau Meet

Genesis 33

The next morning Esau came. Jacob
bowed in fear in front of him. Surprise!
Esau was happy to see Jacob. Esau ran
to Jacob and gave him hugs and kisses.

66

"Who are all these people?" Esau asked. "They are mine," Jacob answered. "God has been good to me." The brothers became friends again.

Do you have brothers and sisters?
Do you treat them kindly?

Deborah

Judges 4:1–16

When the people got settled in their new land, God gave them leaders to help them. One of them was a woman named Deborah. People came to her under a tree, so that she could settle their arguments.

She and her general, Barak, went into battle. Deborah was a brave woman who could win against their enemies. God was on her side.

Deborah was only one of many brave leaders.
Let's see who else was a leader.

Gideon

Judges 6:11–24

One day an angel came to a man named Gideon. The angel said, "The Lord is with you, mighty warrior! Go save God's people."

70

Gideon said, "Not me. My family is the weakest in our tribe, and I am the weakest in our family." The angel said to Gideon, "I will be with you." And that's how Gideon became a leader of God's people.

God doesn't always look for the strongest person to do His work. He looks for people who will do what He asks them to do.

Too Many Soldiers

Judges 6:33–7:8

72

Gideon was scared, but he decided he would do what God asked. He got an army together. God said, "You have too many soldiers." Gideon sent thousands of men home. God said, "You still have too many. Take them to drink water. Keep only those who put water in their hands and lap it like a dog." That left Gideon with only 300 soldiers.

How could Gideon win a war with only 300 soldiers?
Just see what God does next!

Trumpets and Pots

Judges 7:16–22

God told Gideon to give each of his men trumpets and jars. A burning torch was inside each jar.

While the enemy was sleeping, Gideon's men blew their trumpets as loudly as they could. Then they broke their pots and let the fire from the torches shine. The enemy soldiers woke up, and they were so scared they began fighting one another. After a while they ran away.

Because Gideon did what God told him to do, God won the battle for His people! Yea, God!

Samson

Judges 13:1–5, 24–25

One of the leaders of God's people was chosen before he was born.

An angel told the mother, "You will have a son! But you must never cut his hair. His long hair will show that he's a Nazirite—someone who has work to do for God."

76

This baby grew up to be very strong. His name was Samson, and he always won against his enemies.

It's too bad Samson wasn't as smart as he was strong. He was about to get in a bunch of big trouble.

Samson's Haircut

Judges 16:4–21

Samson had a girlfriend. Her name was Delilah. She asked, "What makes you so strong, Samson?" At first he wouldn't tell her. She begged and whined. Finally he said, "If someone shaved my head, I would lose my strength."

When Samson fell asleep, Delilah had someone to shave off his hair. Samson wasn't strong anymore. Now his enemies had no trouble taking him to their prison.

Poor Samson. He wasn't wise when he chose Delilah to be his friend. We need to be careful about the kind of friends we choose.

Pushing the Pillars

Judges 16:23–31

In prison Samson's hair grew long again.
One night his enemies had a party. They
brought Samson in and made fun of him.

Samson asked God to help him once more. And God did. When Samson pushed against the pillars that held up the building, down it all came on top of everyone. Those people would never hurt anyone again.

Samson was the strongest man in the Bible.
Who made him strong?

Ruth and Naomi

Ruth 1

Ruth and Naomi were widows. That means their husbands had died. Ruth had been married to Naomi's son. One day Naomi decided to go back to the land from which her family had come.

Ruth decided to go with her. Naomi thought Ruth might miss her family and friends. She told Ruth not to come with her. But Ruth said, "Don't ask me to leave you!" And so they went together.

Ruth didn't know where she was going, and she didn't know the big surprise waiting for her. Try to guess what it was.

83

Ruth Gathers Grain

Ruth 2

Ruth and Naomi were very poor. They didn't have enough to eat. Naomi was too old to work, so Ruth went out to a rich man's field to gather leftover grain for food. The rich man saw her. She was a beautiful young woman. "Stay here and work in my field," he told her.

Ruth was taking care of Naomi, and God was taking care of them both. But God wasn't finished with His surprise yet. What will it be?

85

Ruth and Boaz

Ruth 3–4

Naomi decided Boaz would be a good husband for Ruth. She told Ruth what she should do to see if Boaz wanted to marry her. Ruth did exactly what Naomi said. Boaz liked Ruth and wanted to marry her. So they were married and had a little boy. That made all of them happy.

God's surprises are always very special if we can just wait for His time to give them to us. Tell about a surprise you've had.

Hannah's Prayer

1 Samuel 1:1–18

One day a woman named Hannah went to God's Holy Tent to pray. She asked God for a baby son. She promised God her son would work for Him all his life. Eli, the priest, saw her praying. He thought there was something wrong. Hannah told him she was very sad and talking to God about her troubles. Eli said, "May the Lord give you what you want." Hannah was not sad anymore.

What do you pray to God about?

Hannah's Boy

1 Samuel 1:19–28; 2:19

Hannah's prayer was answered. She had a baby boy and named him Samuel, which means "God heard."

When Samuel was about three years old, Hannah took him to Eli, the priest at the Holy Tent. Hannah loved Samuel very much. Every year she made him a new coat.

Hannah kept her promise to God by taking Samuel to Eli. God had big plans for Samuel. What do you think they were?

Samuel Listens

1 Samuel 3:1–14

Samuel's job was to help Eli in the Lord's work. One night Samuel ran to where Eli the priest was sleeping. Samuel had heard someone call his name, and he thought it was Eli. "I didn't call you," Eli said. "Go back to bed."

So Samuel went back to bed, but the voice called him two more times. After the third time, Eli knew that God was calling Samuel. Eli told Samuel to say, "Speak, Lord. I'm listening." God told Samuel that He was going to punish Eli's sons because they were evil.

What would you do if God called you in the middle of the night?

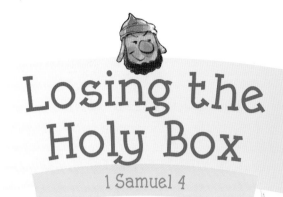

Losing the Holy Box

1 Samuel 4

When Samuel had grown up, there was a war. God's people decided to take the Holy Box into the battle. When they did this, they did not follow God's rules. Guess what? The enemy captured the Holy Box of God and took it home with them. God's people were sad.

God's people knew the rules, but
decided not to follow them.
What do you think about following rules?

95

Coming Home

1 Samuel 5–6:13

As soon as the enemy got the Holy Box of God home, bad things started happening to them. They wanted to get rid of it. They put the Holy Box in a cart pulled by two cows and sent it home. When God's people saw the Holy Box coming, they were so happy!

God's people didn't even have to fight to get the Holy Box back. God will take care of us, even when someone is mean to us.

97

A Scary Thunderclap

1 Samuel 7:2–11

The enemy wasn't quite through yet.
They saw God's people meeting together
and decided to attack them. The people
begged Samuel to pray. He did, and God
sent a thunderclap so loud it frightened
the enemy soldiers. Then God's people
chased them away.

99

Wow! That must have been quite a thunderclap.
God can even use nature to win over evil.

A King for Israel

1 Samuel 8–15

After a while God's people decided they
wanted a king. God didn't think that was
a good idea, but He told Samuel to pour
oil on the head of a tall, young farmer
named Saul. That showed God had
chosen him to be king.

At first Saul let Samuel help him make good decisions. But then Saul decided to do things that made God unhappy. So God decided to let someone else be king in Saul's place. It made Samuel sad to tell Saul that God didn't want him to be king anymore.

Isn't it too bad about Saul? Let's see who God chose to be the next king.

The Youngest Son

1 Samuel 16:1–13

God sent Samuel to the house of a man named Jesse to choose a new king. When Samuel looked at seven of Jesse's sons, God said to him, "Don't look at how tall or handsome they are."

102

"Are these all of your sons?" Samuel asked. Jesse said, "My youngest son is taking care of the sheep. His name is David." God said to Samuel, "David is the one I've chosen."

God doesn't care if you are tall or short or have blue eyes or brown. He just wants you to have a heart that loves Him.

David the Shepherd

1 Samuel 16:11; Psalm 23

David was a shepherd. It was his job to protect and care for sheep. When he was with the sheep, he made up songs and sang them to God. One of those songs says: "The Lord is my shepherd. I have everything that I need."

As David watched the sheep, he became close friends with God.

105

It's good to sing songs to God.
What is your favorite song to sing to Him?

David and the Giant

1 Samuel 17:1–24

God's Holy Spirit came to be with David. It made him brave and strong. One day Jesse told David to go check on his brothers who were soldiers. When David got to the battlefield, he found the soldiers were all afraid of a giant named Goliath. Goliath liked to yell at the soldiers and scare them. He wanted to hurt them.

God gave David courage so he wouldn't
be afraid of the giant. What would you do if
you needed some courage?

Down Goes the Giant

1 Samuel 17:25–58

David wasn't afraid of Goliath. He gathered five smooth small stones and put them in his pouch. Then with his slingshot in one hand, David went to meet Goliath.

The giant laughed when he saw that David was just a boy. But David shot a stone from the slingshot. It hit Goliath in the head and killed him.

David was brave, and he trusted God.
God will help us in scary times if we just ask Him.

King Saul Chases David

1 Samuel 18–23

By killing the giant Goliath, David became a hero. God's people loved him. King Saul became jealous of David and eventually tried to kill him. Saul and his soldiers chased after David and hunted for him everywhere.

But David and the brave men who went with him were protected by God, and Saul couldn't catch them.

Let's see how David gets away from Saul. You may be surprised.

David and Jonathan

1 Samuel 18:1-4; 20

King Saul had a son named Jonathan. Jonathan was a prince. He and David were best friends. He even gave David his coat. Jonathan knew his father wanted to hurt David. So Jonathan helped David run away and hide from Saul. That was a brave thing for Prince Jonathan to do. If David became the next king, Jonathan would never be king of Israel.

113

Best friends help each other. Do you have a best
friend? What could you do to help your friend?

Jonathan's Son

1 Samuel 31; 2 Samuel 1:1–11; 5:1–4; 9

One day King Saul and his son Jonathan died in a battle against the enemy. When David heard this, he was very sad. Soon afterward, David became king. He always took care of his best friend Jonathan's son Mephibosheth. Mephibosheth was crippled in both feet.

David loved God and wanted to please Him.
But one time David made a big mistake.
Let's see what happened.

115

David Does Wrong

2 Samuel 11–12:13; Psalm 51

David usually went to war with his soldiers. But one time he stayed home and got into big trouble. He took another man's wife as his own. The woman's name was Bathsheba. Then David sent the man into battle to be killed. That was wrong!

When David realized how wrong he had been, he was truly sorry. He asked God to forgive him, and God did.

God will forgive us if we are truly sorry for what we've done wrong and ask His forgiveness.

A Wise Woman

2 Samuel 20:1, 14–22

Joab, David's general, and the army were trying to catch a troublemaker. They were digging under the wall of a city to make it fall down. Then a wise woman inside the city called down to Joab, "What are you doing?"

"We're trying to capture a troublemaker,"
Joab said. The wise woman told the city
leaders that there was a troublemaker
hiding in their city. So the leaders
captured and killed the bad man. When
Joab heard this, he took his army and
went home. The city was saved.

We don't even know this lady's name, but we
remember her because she was brave.

Two Kingdoms

1 Kings 12:20; 16:29–33; 17:1

After Samuel, David, and Solomon
died, God's people were split into two
kingdoms—Israel in the north and Judah
in the south. King Ahab ruled Israel.
He did many things that God said were
wrong. He worshiped idols and did more
evil than any of the kings before him.

So God sent Elijah, the prophet, to teach Ahab a lesson. Elijah told Ahab that there would be no rain for many years. This made Ahab very angry.

Ahab and his wife, Jezebel, wanted to kill Elijah. But God wanted him to live. Let's see how God protected Elijah.

Elijah Runs Away from King Ahab

1 Kings 17:7–15

Elijah had to run away from Ahab and camp near a brook. God sent birds to bring the prophet food.

When the brook dried up, God told Elijah
to go ask a certain woman for food.
"I only have enough left for one meal
for me and my son," she said. Elijah
said, "Cook for me first, and you'll be all
right." So she did.

**The woman believed what Elijah said,
and guess what? After she fed Elijah,
she never ran out of food.**

Whose God Is Real?

1 Kings 18:1, 15–24

Three years passed with no rain. Finally, God told Elijah to go meet King Ahab. "There you are, you big troublemaker," said the king. But it was really the king who had caused the trouble.

"Let's see whose god is real," Elijah said. So the king's prophets built one altar to their god, and Elijah built an altar to his God. They put offerings on each of them. Then they prayed and waited to see whose god would answer their prayers by sending fire to burn up the sacrifice.

What do you suppose Elijah was up to?

Fire from Heaven

1 Kings 18:25–46

The king's prophets screamed at their fake gods to send fire. No fire came. Elijah teased, "Pray louder." They did. But nothing happened. When they stopped, Elijah had water poured over everything on the altar he'd built. Then he prayed to God in heaven to send fire.

Fire came down. It burned up the offering, the stones, and the water. Then the people knew Elijah's God was the most powerful.

When Elijah prayed again, it began to rain.
How do you think the king felt about that?

Elijah in the Desert

1 Kings 19:1–8

Even though rain had come, King Ahab and his evil wife, Jezebel, still wanted to kill Elijah. Elijah ran for his life to the desert. He was so tired he lay right down and went to sleep.

Soon someone tapped him on the shoulder. An angel had come to make Elijah dinner. The angel fed Elijah a second time too. Then Elijah was strong enough to make a long journey.

What do you suppose Elijah thought when an angel brought him food?

God Speaks to Elijah

1 Kings 19:9–18

Elijah was still being chased by the evil king, and that made Elijah sad. Elijah went into a cave. God said, "Stand here and I will pass by." A strong wind blew, but God didn't speak. An earthquake shook the ground, but God didn't speak.

A fire burned, but still God didn't speak.
Then when it was quiet, Elijah heard
the gentle voice of God. "Go find a man
named Elisha. He will be a helper to you,
and he will be the next prophet."

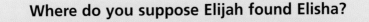

Where do you suppose Elijah found Elisha?

Elijah's Helper

1 Kings 19:19–21

Elijah left the desert right away. He found Elisha plowing a field. Elijah put his coat over the young man. That meant he wanted Elisha to be his helper. First Elisha and his family had a big feast. Then he said good-bye to his mother and father and followed Elijah.

133

Elijah did exactly what God told him to do. Now he and Elisha would work for God together.

A Bad Queen

1 Kings 21–22:39

King Ahab and his evil wife, Jezebel, decided they wanted a neighbor's land. Speaking badly against God or the king was against the law. Jezebel got some people to lie and say the neighbor, Naboth, had said bad things about both God and King Ahab.

So Jezebel had Naboth killed, and King Ahab took Naboth's land. Not long afterward King Ahab and his wife both died terrible deaths.

God saw what Ahab and Jezebel had done. How do you think that made God feel?

Chariot of Fire

2 Kings 2:1–12

Elijah was getting old. His helper, Elisha, went with him everywhere.

One day Elijah and Elisha were together when God sent a chariot and horses made of fire. The fiery horses and chariot came between Elijah and Elisha. Then *whoosh!* All of a sudden Elijah went up to heaven in a whirlwind. Elisha saw him go.

Someday we will go to heaven. It will be a wonderful place. Who do you think we'll see there?

Captured!

2 Kings 24:18–25:21; 2 Chronicles 36:15–23

Over and over God had warned His people not to worship idols. But they kept right on doing what God had told them not to do. So finally God let an enemy capture His people and take them from the land He'd given them. They were taken far away to a place called Babylon. It was a sad day.

God wants us to do what is right, and He is very patient. But if we continue to do wrong, we will have to suffer the consequences.

139

Beautiful Queen Esther

Esther 1–3

Years later the Persian kingdom defeated Babylon. But God's people were still living in the land of Babylon. One of them was a young woman named Esther.

The king of Persia wanted a beautiful young woman to be his queen. He picked Esther. Soon afterward one of the king's men decided to get rid of all God's people in the kingdom. Since Esther was one of them, it meant he would get rid of her too.

It must have been a very scary time for Esther.
What do you think she did?

Esther Saves Her People

Esther 4–9

Esther knew it was up to her to save her people. She also knew that if she visited the king and he got angry, she wouldn't be queen anymore. The king could even have her killed. What should she do?

142

Esther decided to go to the king anyway. When she went, the king granted her wish that her people would be allowed to live.

Esther was very brave. She did what God wanted her to do, and because she was brave, she saved her people. Yea, Esther!

Three Brave Men

Daniel 3:1–23

Remember how God's people were captured and taken away to the country of Babylon? The king of that country was Nebuchadnezzar. Three of these young men—Shadrach, Meshach, and Abednego—worked for King Nebuchadnezzar.

But when the king wanted them to bow down and worship a golden idol, they wouldn't do it. So the king told his soldiers to put all three men into a red-hot furnace.

God was pleased that these young men loved Him so much they would not worship the king's idol. What do you think happened next?

The Extra Man

Daniel 3:24–30

Guess what? The men in the furnace didn't burn up. God sent someone to protect them in the furnace. The king was surprised when he saw four people walking around. He told Shadrach, Meshach, and Abednego to come out of the furnace.

Then the king made a new law. It said that no one could say anything bad about the God of these men.

God has promised to be with us
no matter what happens to us.

New
Testament

An Angel's Message

Luke 1:5–20

A priest named Zachariah went to God's house to burn an incense offering. As soon as he was inside, the angel Gabriel appeared. "Zachariah, you and your wife, Elizabeth, will have a son. You will name him John," Gabriel said.

Zachariah didn't believe it was possible for Elizabeth and him to have a son. They were too old. "Because you don't believe me, Zachariah, you will not be able to talk until the baby is born," Gabriel said.

John was going to be a very important person. He would tell others to get ready because Jesus was coming.

A Baby Named John

Luke 1:57–66

Just as the angel Gabriel had said, a baby boy was born to Zachariah and his wife, Elizabeth.

Their friends were very happy for them.
"Name him Zachariah after his father,"
they said. Zachariah still couldn't talk,
so he wrote down, "His name is John." As
soon as Zachariah wrote that, he could
talk again.

His name
is John.

People don't get to see angels very often,
but when they do, they need to pay attention.
Angels bring messages from God. What is
another way God sends messages?

Mary's Big Surprise

Luke 1:26–38

Not long after his visit to Zachariah, the angel Gabriel went to see a young woman named Mary. She was a cousin to Elizabeth, Zachariah's wife. Mary lived in Nazareth and was engaged to marry Joseph, the carpenter.

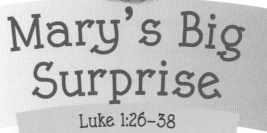

"Don't be afraid, Mary," the angel said. "God is pleased with you. You will have a baby and will name Him Jesus. He will be called the Son of God." This was a big surprise to Mary.

What would you do if an angel suddenly appeared right here in front of you?

Joseph Marries Mary

Matthew 1:18–25

When Joseph heard the news that Mary was going to have a baby, he didn't know what to think. He wasn't married to her yet. God loved Joseph and wanted him to understand that the baby was from God and everything was going to be all right.

So God sent an angel to talk to Joseph in a dream. This angel told Joseph, "Name the baby Jesus. He will save people from their sins." When Joseph heard God's plan, he married Mary.

The name *Jesus* means "savior."
What does a savior do?

God's Baby Son

Luke 2:1–7

The ruler of the land, Augustus Caesar, made a new law to count all the people. Everyone had to register in their hometown. So Joseph and Mary went to their hometown, Bethlehem. The town was full of people. There was no place for Mary and Joseph to sleep.

Finally, Joseph found a place for them where the animals were kept. And that's where God's Baby Son was born. His first bed was on the hay in the box where the animals were fed.

Why do you think God would want His Son to be born where the animals were kept?

Some Sleepy Shepherds

Luke 2:8–12

That night, out in the fields, sleepy shepherds were taking care of their sheep. Suddenly an angel appeared in the sky. The angel's light was so bright, it hurt their eyes.

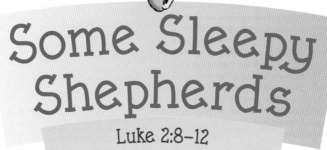

160

"Don't be afraid," the angel said. "I have good news for you. A baby was born in Bethlehem town tonight. He is your Savior. You will find Him lying in a feeding box."

Who was the first to hear about Baby Jesus?

What the Shepherds Saw

Luke 2:13–20

Then the whole sky filled
up with so many angels
no one could count them
all. They sang, "Glory
to God in heaven!"
And then, when the
song was over,
the angels
disappeared.

The shepherds hurried to Bethlehem. They found Mary and Joseph and saw Baby Jesus lying in the hay in the feeding box. The shepherds told them everything the angels had said about the child.

If you had been out there on the hill with the shepherds, what would you have been thinking when the angels left?

Gifts for Baby Jesus

Matthew 2:1–12

Soon many of the people who came to register in Bethlehem went home. Mary and Joseph moved into a house.

One day they had visitors who came from far away in the east. These visitors were wise men. They had followed a bright star to find little Jesus. They bowed down and worshiped God's only Son and gave Him expensive presents of gold, frankincense, and myrrh.

165

Why do you think the wise men came to see little Jesus?

Another Journey

Matthew 2:13–15

After the wise men left, God sent another angel to Joseph in a dream. "Take the child and Mary and go to Egypt," the angel said. "King Herod wants to kill Jesus. Stay in Egypt until I tell you it's safe to come home."

It was still night, but Joseph got up out of bed and took Mary and Jesus and headed for Egypt.

Joseph obeyed God immediately. And God kept his family safe. Why is it good to obey quickly?

Home at Last!

Mary, Joseph, and Jesus stayed in Egypt until God sent another angel to Joseph in a dream. "Get up and take Mary and Jesus and go home," said the angel. King Herod had died. He could never hurt them again. God and His angels had kept Mary, Joseph, and Jesus safe.

So with happy hearts, they went home to live in Nazareth.

Whew! It was finally safe to go home. How do you think Mary and Joseph felt about that?

The Man Who Ate Locusts

Matthew 3:1–13; Mark 1:4–9

Jesus' cousin, John, became a preacher when he grew up. He lived in the desert and wore rough clothes and ate locusts and honey. (Locusts were like grasshoppers.) John told the people to change their hearts and lives and ask forgiveness for their wrongs because Jesus was coming soon.

One day when Jesus was grown up, too, He came to the place where John was preaching and baptizing people. Jesus asked John to baptize Him in the river.

When Jesus asked John to baptize Him,
do you think John did it?

John Baptizes Jesus

Matthew 3:13–17

At first John didn't want to baptize Jesus. He thought Jesus should be the one to baptize *him*. But when Jesus said it needed to be this way, John obeyed and took Jesus into the river and baptized Him.

As Jesus came up out of the water, God's Spirit, like a dove, came down to Him from heaven. God spoke and said, "This is My Son, and I love Him. I am very pleased with Him."

Jesus set a good example for us by following God's command to be baptized. Have you been baptized?

Jesus Tempted by Satan

Matthew 4:1–4

Soon God's Spirit led Jesus away from the river and into the desert. Jesus wanted to pray and think about what God wanted Him to do next. Jesus fasted—that means He didn't eat, so He got very hungry. Then the devil, Satan, appeared. Satan knew that Jesus was tired and hungry.

"Turn these rocks into bread," Satan told Jesus. Jesus knew that Satan was trying to get Him to do something wrong. Jesus had studied God's Word, so He remembered what He had learned from the Scriptures. He said, "A person does not live only by eating bread. A person lives by doing everything the Lord says."

Satan doesn't stop picking on people with just one try. He was not through with Jesus yet. Keep reading to see what happened next.

On Top of the Temple

Matthew 4:5–7

Satan took Jesus to Jerusalem and stood Him on the very top of the Temple. The Temple is where God's people worshiped. "If you are God's Son, jump down from this high place," Satan said. "It is written in the Scriptures that God's angels will catch You." That was not a smart thing for Satan to suggest, and Jesus knew it. He answered by saying, "It is also written in the Scriptures, 'Do not test God.'"

177

It is foolish to test or tease God. Testing God means doing very risky things that might get you hurt.

The Kingdoms of the World

Matthew 4:8-11

That sneaky devil, Satan, had one more test up his sleeve. He took Jesus to a high mountain and showed Him all the kingdoms of the world. Satan said, "Bow down and give honor to me, and I will give You all these things."

Jesus had an answer ready, "Go away from Me! It is written in the Scriptures, 'You must worship only the Lord God.'" So Satan went away.

Even though we can't see Satan, he tries to get us to do things that are wrong. What are some of the things Satan tries to get us to do?

Jesus Heals
a Sick Boy

John 4:46–51

Jesus loved little children, and whenever He could, He helped them. One day an important man begged Jesus to come to his house and heal his sick son. But Jesus didn't go. Instead He said, "Go home. Your son will live."

180

The man believed Jesus and went home, but before he got there his servants met him and said, "Your son is well."

When we believe and trust someone to do something we cannot see, that is called *faith*. The man in this story trusted Jesus to keep a promise. Whom do you trust?

Jesus Brings a Girl Back to Life

Mark 5:22–43

Jesus also helped a little girl. Her father's name was Jairus, and he was an important man. "My little daughter is dying," Jairus said. "Please come and pray for her so she will get well and live." Before Jesus could go to the little girl, she died. But Jesus went anyway. With the child's mother and father and three of His followers, Jesus went in the girl's room and took her hand in His. "Little girl," Jesus said, "stand up!" And she did. She was well.

When we ask God for something, sometimes He says yes, and sometimes He says no. The most important thing is that He always hears us.

183

A Little Boy
Helps Jesus

John 6:1–13

Great crowds of people followed Jesus
to see His miracles and hear Him teach
about God's love for them. The people
sometimes forgot to take food with
them. One day a huge crowd of 5,000 men
and their families followed Jesus. It was
late in the day when they reached Jesus,
and the people were getting hungry.

The only one with any food was a little boy with five small loaves of bread and two fish. Jesus blessed the food. His closest followers and helpers gave it to the people. After everyone had plenty to eat, the helpers gathered up 12 baskets of leftover food.

185

What do you have that you could give Jesus? An offering? Some time to help someone?

Jesus Loves Children

Luke 18:15–17

Many people wanted to see Jesus. When Jesus saw how sick and sad they were, He wanted to help them. One day some people brought their children to Him. His helpers tried to send them away. Jesus said, "Let the little children come to Me. Don't stop them. You must love and accept God like a little child if you want to enter heaven."

187

If you were one of the children who got to sit on
Jesus' lap, what would you say to Him?

One Lost Sheep

Luke 15:3–7

Here is a story Jesus told. A man had 100 sheep, but he lost one. Now, what was he going to do? He left his 99 sheep safe at home and went looking for the one lost sheep.

He searched everywhere, and when he finally found the lost sheep, he was so happy. He put the sheep on his shoulders and carried it home.

How is Jesus like that shepherd looking for his one lost sheep? Remember, you are as important to Jesus as that one lost sheep was to the shepherd.

A Son Spends All His Money

Luke 15:11-13

Jesus told another story. A man had two sons. The younger son said, "Give me my share of the property and money." So the father divided the property and money between his younger son and older son.

The younger man went to another country far away. He had lots of fun spending every bit of his money.

Do you think the younger son was making a good decision? How do you think his father felt?

The Man Who Ate Pig Food

Luke 15:14–19

After the younger son's money was gone, he got very hungry. A man gave him a job feeding pigs. As the son fed the pigs, he was so hungry that he ate the pig food.

After a while he began to realize he had been very foolish. He said to himself, "My father's servants have plenty of food. I'm going home. I'll tell my father that I have done wrong. I'll ask him if I can just be a servant."

Wow, what a mess! What were some of the choices the son made that got him into a pigpen?

Going Home to Father

Luke 15:20–32

The younger son went home. He was worried that his father wouldn't want him. But his father had been looking for him every day for a long time.

194

When he saw his son, the father ran to meet him. He hugged him and gave him new clothes. He had a party to welcome him home. He told everyone, "My son was lost, but now he is found!"

The father in this story is like God. God sees us make bad choices, and He is sad. But He is always waiting for us to come back to Him.

A Mean Man

Acts 9:1-4

There was a mean man chasing after Jesus' followers. His name was Saul. He was sure that everything he heard about Jesus was wrong. He didn't believe any of it. He was sure he was right. So he hurt, and even killed, people who believed in Jesus.

Well, God wanted Saul to work for Him. So one day when Saul was on a journey, God sent a bright flash of light. It was so bright, Saul fell to the ground.

Why do you think God wanted Saul to work for Him?

Saul Is Blinded

Acts 9:4–9

"Saul! Why are you doing things against Me?" a voice said from inside the light. "Who are you?" asked Saul. "I am Jesus. Now get up and go into the city."

When Saul stood up, he was blind. His friends had to lead him into the city. Saul wouldn't eat or drink anything for three days.

199

What will happen to poor, blind Saul? Do you think he is ready to listen to God?

Ananias Helps Saul

Acts 9:10–18; 13:9

God sent a man named Ananias to find Saul and pray for him so that Saul could see again. Ananias was scared of Saul. But Ananias believed in Jesus and went anyway.

200

Ananias prayed for Saul, and Saul's sight came back. On that day, God changed Saul's heart to make him kind to those who believed in Jesus. Saul was also called Paul. Soon Paul began to tell others about Jesus too.

Did you know that Paul became one of the greatest preachers who ever lived?

A Woman Who Sold Purple Cloth

Acts 16:12–15

After Paul became a follower of Jesus, he went everywhere teaching people about Jesus. Many times there was no building where he could meet with friends. One day he and his friends were looking for a place to meet by the river when they saw a group of women.

One woman was Lydia. Her job was selling purple cloth. She loved God, but didn't know about Jesus. Paul told her all about Jesus, and Lydia believed that Jesus was God's Son. Lydia invited Paul and his friends to stay at her house.

Some of your friends probably want to know Jesus. They are just waiting for someone to tell them about Him. You could be the one who tells them.

Earthquake!

Acts 16:16–36

Some people didn't like what Paul was preaching about Jesus. So they caught Paul and his helper, Silas, and threw them in jail. The two men were beaten, and their feet were fastened tightly so they couldn't run away. That night, instead of complaining or crying, Paul and Silas prayed and sang songs to God.

Suddenly there was an earthquake, and the jail doors popped open. The jailer thought his prisoners had escaped. He knew if the prisoners had escaped, he would be in big trouble. Paul called to him, "We are all here!" When the jailer came to them, he asked, "What must I do to be saved?" Paul told him all about Jesus.

If you had been beaten, thrown in jail, and had your feet pinned down, what would you be doing?

Some People Laugh at Paul

Acts 17:16–34

Paul traveled to Athens in Greece to tell people about Jesus. In Athens, Paul saw an altar with writing that said, "TO A GOD WHO IS NOT KNOWN." Paul began to preach. He told the people about the God who made the whole world.

Paul said that God doesn't live in temples that men build, but in their hearts. He told them about Jesus coming back to life after being dead. Some of the people laughed at Paul, but some of the people believed in Jesus.

TO A GOD WHO IS NOT KNOWN.

God wants all of us to tell others the Good News that Jesus is alive. Some people will believe, and some will laugh. We must pray for all of them.

Shipwrecked!

Acts 27

Paul got on a big ship. He was going to the city of Rome. The ship went very slowly because of strong winds blowing against it. Finally, the ship came to a safe harbor, and Paul told the captain he didn't think it was a good idea to leave the harbor for a while. But the captain disagreed, and he sailed anyway.

Soon a wind came up and blew hard on the ship. The sailors couldn't steer it. Paul knew they were in trouble—they might sink. He told the sailors to eat so they would be strong for the trouble ahead. Before long, the ship hit a sandbank and began to break into pieces. Everyone had to jump into the sea and swim for the beach. They all made it to shore safely.

How scary! A shipwreck! Where did they land?
What happened next?

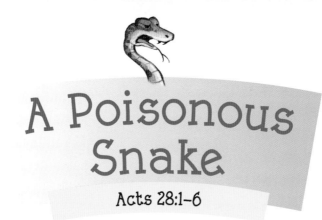

A Poisonous Snake

Acts 28:1–6

All the people from the shipwreck were now on the island of Malta, near the country of Greece. The people who lived on the island were very kind. They built a fire and invited the passengers to warm themselves.

Paul helped by gathering wood for the fire, and as he did, a poisonous snake bit him on the hand. Paul just shook the snake off into the fire. He was not even hurt. The island people waited for him to fall down dead from the poison, but Paul was just fine.

Why do you think Paul did not die when the poisonous snake bit him?

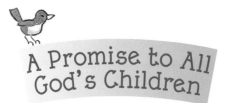

A Promise to All God's Children

"No one has ever seen this.
No one has ever heard about it.
No one has ever imagined
what God has prepared
for those who love him."

1 Corinthians 2:9

Bringing the Bible to life for your little ones with **Read and Share**®

Packed with 200 stories, *The Read and Share® Bible* is sure to win the hearts of little ones and give them a strong Bible foundation.

The Read and Share® Toddler Bible offers 40 stories plus a 60-minute DVD for even the littlest of God's children.

The Read and Share® DVD Bible series builds a foundation in knowing God's Word in young minds. Collection includes 52, 3-minute Bible stories in bold, bright animation.

Straight from the pages of the popular *Read and Share® Bible*, The Jesus Series walks children though the birth, life, death and resurrection of Christ.

Learn more about *Read and Share*®!
www.TommyNelson.com